Reality Check:
A College Student's Survival Guide

by

John Mikaelian

This information in this publication is not intended to replace or substitute advice provided by your instructors, physicians, or counselors.

Copyright © 2012 by Hovannes John Mikaelian. All rights reserved. This book or any portion thereof may not be reproduced or used in any manner whatsoever without the express written permission of Hovannes John Mikaelian.

Printed in the United States of America

ISBN 978-0-9904456-0-9 (U.S.)

www.johnmikaelian.com

Contents

Introduction 1

Chapter 1: 'Like' My Status 5

Chapter 2: You Want to Be Cool, Right?.......... 21

Chapter 3: Food For Thought 39

Chapter 4: Swipe Responsibly 65

Chapter 5: Dollars and Sense 87

Chapter 6: Making the Grade 105

Chapter 7: Tech-know-logic Lifestyles 131

Introduction

As a college student, I've never been a big fan of reading. For some reason, all the academic and non-fiction books I've read contained vocabulary and phrases that were strange to me. I would either be forced to stop reading and put the book down to look up each term or would have to make a note of it and look them up later. In my opinion, that process stole some of the pleasure from the whole reading experience. Why did it seem difficult to create readable material that could be understood in a single reading yet contain a significant, challenging message? I have always felt there has been a void for books that possess a simple writing style yet transmit the writer's powerful thoughts to the reader. After all, a book is only as good as the author's message to the reader.

When it came to writing essays, I was always taught to write the way I spoke. Sticking to that philosophy, I have attempted to apply my own expectations to the style for this book. Much like blogs you might have stumbled upon on the Internet, the first thing you will notice in these pages is that the sentences are fluid and the words flow naturally, almost as if you and I are having a conversation. You may also notice that I have tried to eliminate (or at least reduce) the "academic" style of formatting and expression. After reading a few pages, you might think that you're reading a magazine or a news article rather than a book.

Growing up, I didn't have an older brother or anyone to look up to, no one around me to make the first mistakes so I could see what to avoid. I was clueless on which direction to walk and which path to take. I learned all of life's lessons through trial and error. Sure, it would've been a lot easier if I had someone teaching me right from wrong. However, would it have been more rewarding than figuring things out for myself?

Having a passion for writing music and helping people, I've always wanted to reach out to as many people as I can and share some of my experiences through music but who knows how long that would take. Finding a record label deal and promoting an album can take a while. So, I asked myself, "What's another way I can reach out to a large audience and connect with them?" Of course, write a book! Now, writing a book and writing music are two different things but at the end of the day, both a listener and a reader are interested in what the artist/author has to say. Never in a million years would I have imagined myself writing a book. I made my best attempt to provide my message to my readers as clearly as possible.

With that being said, I wrote this book based on the knowledge I gained through my personal experiences. Everyone can use a hand every once in a while, regardless if they asked for it or not. When one door closes, another door opens. You will find a lot of information that you can relate to. You may be experiencing some of the same problems as I did.

I personally wanted to thank you, the reader, in advance for taking the time to read my book. I strongly believe that you will find something that you can take from this book and apply it to your own life. Perhaps, you will find answers to some of the same questions I had before I wrote this book. What are the pros and cons of social media? What are some of the unpleasant realities our generation faces as they head off to young adulthood? How can we, college students, stay healthy both physically and mentally? How are college students supposed to manage their credit and finances? How does a college student balance work and school? Is it important to have a college degree in today's world? Finally, how has technology impacted our current generation in terms of lifestyle and employment in the near future? Anyways, without further ado, I present to you *Reality Check: A College Student's Survival Guide.* Enjoy!

1
'Like' My Status

It's no secret that social media has grown quickly over the past few years, and the activity with which it surrounds us is very compelling to the say the least. Social media can be thought of as the friend who lives next door and knows you very well. It knows when you're happy and when you're upset. It knows who you talk to and recommends people for you to talk to. Our spirits are filled with curiosity and eagerness the moment we find out there's new activity begging for our attention. It's almost as if we are enjoying a moment from our childhood when we used to go to the candy store and indulge on our favorite sweets; we savored the moment and hoped it would last forever.

As you may already know, however, good things don't last forever including our childhood memories. You're probably staring at me like a deer blinded by bright headlights wondering what the heck I'm talking about but bear with me here and we'll get to the good stuff. Have you ever noticed how notifications appear? They pop out on the screen with attractive colors and designs. For some reason, it reminds me of the bright lights you see in Las Vegas. There's no denying that they are there to grab our attention but how much of our attention do we devote to social media? Are we spending too much time on social networks? Are we too dependent on them?

    I'm sure you've heard this a couple times from your parents before. Alright, let's be honest, I'm sure you've heard this many, many times before. Parents are always wondering what we, young adults, are doing on social networks. For example, my parents always tell me how they didn't have this type of digital communication when they were my age. If I had a dime for every time I heard that, I would be standing next to Mark Zuckerberg right now. You know what's interesting? We're always under the impression of how our parents are "anti-social". However, is that true? Are we so social to the point where our parents are anti-social? If you think about it, someone who is anti-social would be someone that doesn't really put his or her self out there and interact with people face to face.

Technically, when we send messages through these social networks, we are communicating with others but it's not being done in person. So would that make us anti-social even though we are communicating with others through social networks? You have to understand where our parents and ancestors come from. They lived in a world where they had to depend on one another to spread any type of news whether it was business-related, gossip, marriage invitation, graduation ceremony, you name it. There was something called "word of mouth" back in those days and apparently, it didn't make it into today's world. You might've heard of it before. They used to get together and surround themselves with family and friends, which resulted into storytelling and laughter. When they wanted to watch a movie, they had to go to a movie theatre. Back then, they didn't have the luxuries we enjoy today. They weren't able to watch movies at home on a disc or over the Internet. Nowadays, technology has provided us with many conveniences. In this case,
it's social media. How social is social media,

though? Yes, it allows us to meet new people and reconnect with the ones that we might've lost touch with. It allows us to be social without actually going somewhere. Let's compare apples to apples: let's say you meet someone for the first time on a social network and on the same day, you meet someone else in person. Which scenario would you consider to be more social than the other? I can't make the decision for you as everyone is entitled to their own opinion but it does give you a chance to look deeper into the grand scheme of things.

    No matter where you go, you can't help but notice people constantly checking their social network accounts for new activity whether it's on their cell phones, laptops, or other electronic devices. I have to admit that I have been caught red handed and I am guilty of this as well. I'm sure many of you can relate to that. This doesn't surprise me, though. Social media is a powerful tool that allows you to connect to many people throughout the world who share some of the same interests as you. Social networks allow you to establish connections with new people and share ideas with one another. If you have a great idea, you can spread the word almost instantly.

Since we're already on the subject, let's talk about communication, the "old school way." Since social media, e-mail, text messaging didn't exist a couple of decades ago, people used to talk on the phone. Nothing special about that, right? What about the value of actually being able to hear someone's voice and tone? When you speak to someone on the phone, you can find out a lot of things such as how they're feeling and what type of mood they're in. You would know when they are happy or upset. Also, there's something special about hearing someone's voice. If you haven't talked to a certain individual for a long period of time, you would enjoy talking to them and actually hearing their voice. I might be sounding crazy right now but I'm sure I'm not the only one who feels this way.

When it comes to social media and other forms of electronic text communication, you can't prove the person you're communicating with is the person you assume to be. For example, let's say your friend Natalie just broke up with her boyfriend Jason and she is texting you about the situation. You're her really good friend, so you are texting her back about your opinion of the break-up, of Jason, of everything. You're assuming the person who is sending, reading and replying to your texts is Natalie, right? It very well could be Jason being nosy and pretending to be Natalie. Jason could be very well attempting to obtain information from you and you wouldn't be aware of it. It's more common than you think. My intent is not to make you paranoid but to give you an idea of how valuable it is to speak to someone rather than communicating through a text message, e-mail, or a social media website. Could it be that communication has taken one step forward but five steps back? The latest craze isn't always the greatest depending on your own perspective.

One of my biggest concerns about the digital world has always been security. How secure is your private information on these social networks? Where is all of your private information being stored? Who has access to your information? Word on the street is that prospective employers may have been able to gain access to information posted by potential employees on these social networks. What's the reasoning behind this? Well, employers might be able to dig up information about a job applicant who they believe is a perfect fit for the position they're trying to fill. Any type of information can quickly tip the scale that isn't in favor of the job applicant. Apparently, a résumé does not provide them with sufficient information. Yes, they do have your work experience and background information but quite frankly, it's not enough. What type of information could they be searching for? Your guess is a good as mine as it remains a mystery. They might be looking for photos? Maybe they're taking a peak at the status updates you post to see how you communicate with others? Whatever the case may be, it wouldn't be a bad idea to take some security precautions. Lately, I've noticed a lot of pictures being used by the news media that are directly from social networks. The source of the picture is usually cited underneath the picture. I guess that's one way to appear on TV, right?

On a serious note, you would be surprised to find out who has access to your information. Once you have posted media content on these social networks, it's pretty much public record. You might want to think twice before you "share" photos or other information about the concert or party you went to last night. If it's something you would only want your friends to know about, then you're probably better off not posting it at all.

Speaking of friends, one of the books I read in my English 1A class at Pasadena City College educated me on this topic and allowed me to look at it from a different perspective. I could honestly say that it has changed my life and the way I look at social media. In the book, *Self-Reliance and Other Essays*, there's a chapter where the author, Ralph Waldo Emerson, discusses the true meaning of friendship. He explains the difference between a true friend and a regular friend. According to Emerson, a true friend is someone who is always there for you when you need them the most. A true friend is someone who you see often and spend time with. Who would've guessed, right? Check this out, though. What about the people that we still call friends but rarely see them? They are still there when we need them but do not feel comfortable enough to share our secrets and emotions. Should we still consider them as our friends? In his book, Emerson's concept of a friend only applies to the people that we see a few times a month as opposed to few times a year. Here's the catch, though: in order for someone to be considered a friend, there must be human contact. Someone who we keep in touch with but do not visit often is not considered a friend. So would this hold true to our "friends" on social networks?

In our class discussion at Pasadena City College, we concluded that the people we spend time with the most in person are considered as our friends and people that we communicate with over the Internet are acquaintances. Just because we communicate with them doesn't automatically qualify them as our friends. Are we forced to believe that the people we communicate with through social networks are our friends? This doesn't necessarily apply to the people we communicate with through social networks and see them often in person but what about the people we've never met in person? After all, that's the power of social media. It allows you to meet new people throughout the world but should that be considered as a disadvantage as well?

Friendships take time to develop and the foundation is built on trust. However, by referring to people we meet online as friends, should we TRUST them with our PRIVATE information? After all, they are our friends, right? See the connection here? I found this to be a really interesting concept. You can be the judge of this and draw your own conclusion but as far as I'm concerned, it should not be taken lightly.

It's no surprise that many of us have social network accounts and use them daily. But what about the people who can't afford to purchase the devices that provide them access to social network accounts? With everything social media has to offer, would they be excluded from reaping the benefits? Or what about the people who choose not to create a social network account? Are they going to get left behind? Technology is a convenience and convenience comes with a price tag. While many of us are able to afford the devices that allow us to maintain our social network accounts, there are people out there who still don't have access to the Internet. What are they supposed to do? Are they supposed to feel guilty and look at the glass half empty? Or should they carry on with their lives as if social media never existed?

Curious about what it's like living in today's world without participating in social media, I had the pleasure of speaking to a few friends about it. When I asked them why they didn't have a social network account, they said they didn't see a need in having one. They also stated that their friends pressured them to join the social media world. One thing that really stood out to me was that they put a lot of emphasis on privacy. They strongly believed that social media exposes one's personal life. Everyone has access to who and where you spend most of your time and that made them feel uncomfortable. When they need to talk to their friends, they either send them a text message or call them. And if that wasn't enough, they put the exclamation point by stating that the conversations they have with others belong to them, not for others to find out.

I can see where they're coming from and why they would feel that way. Sometimes, I feel the same way too. For example, I remember that one time I had promised a friend that I would spend some time with him but instead, a once in a lifetime opportunity presented itself. One of my other friends was able to pull a rabbit out of a hat and get two tickets to a concert last minute. Of course, I didn't want to miss out on the concert and in order to not seem like a complete jerk to my other friend for flaking on him, I told him that I came down with a fever. We agreed to postpone our plans.

Long story short, my other friend and I went to the concert and had a great time but that's not how the day ended. The friend that I had gone to the concert with wasn't aware of the situation and posted some pictures on my profile that we had taken at the concert. Before I knew it, the friend that I had bailed on saw the pictures and sent me a text cursing me out. Needless to say, I felt horrible. Social media is great for spreading the word but it can also backfire. This is the reason why many people don't want to maintain a social network account; they don't want to get involved with drama. They might be receiving criticism from their friends for "living under a rock" but the truth is, everyone is allowed to have choices and social media is no exception. It can definitely open a can of worms when you least expect it.

    Again, social media is a powerful tool and a great advancement in technology. It goes to show how innovative and capable technology really is. It could very well be setting the standard on communication whether it's for personal or business use. However, everyone is entitled to their own opinion, as decisions derive from the choices available to us. It's similar to eating ice cream; there are so many flavors to choose from and not everyone will end up choosing the same flavor. Before you sign up for a social network account, you should think about the advantages and the disadvantages. Think of how it would fit into your lifestyle. If the pros outweigh the cons, you may be able to take advantage of all the benefits social media has to offer. However, social media isn't for everyone, as it can draw unwanted attention. What I recommend is to be careful with the information you post online for many reasons. I would have to say security is the biggest reason to avoid posting personal information. By not posting personal information, are you representing yourself with inaccurate information to the people you meet and communicate with online thus defeating the purpose of creating a social network account in the first place?

2
You Want to Be Cool, Right?

Life of a young adult can be very exciting. There are lots of places to go and people to meet. You make a lot of new friends while losing some of your closest ones. You spend your whole week planning for the weekend whether it's for a party, concert, a date, or whatever you're into at the moment. While some people might not be able to take a day off from being a social bug, many others often feel they have to meet the expectations set by their friends. After all, the last thing you want your friends to assume is that you want to disappear from the face of the planet to isolate yourself in a tiny cave and come back as a crime fighting hero with a name influenced by bats. I'm sure you know which character I'm referring to…

Speaking of crime fighting, one of the biggest enemies known to the "average Joe" is peer pressure. It's a powerful force that alters your state of mind and causes you to develop thoughts of uncertainty pertaining to your identity. I guess one way of protecting your identity would be to come out of a telephone booth wearing glasses and a black tuxedo, right? Okay, that might've not been at the top of your list but why is it that we, young adults and college students, put so much emphasis on having a social life?

There are many reasons for submitting to the "herd" mentality. Sometimes, one's personal worth and popularity is measured through their social abilities. Observers may ask, "Who does he/she hang out with", "Why was he/she talking with so and so?", or "Why was he/she not at so and so's party?" and so forth. Why do we create and surround ourselves with so much drama? Why is it that we worry about what others are doing with their lives when we should be concerned about what we do with our own? Could it be that there's a desire to judge others due to our own insecurities?

Nonetheless, living up to your friends' expectations and answering to your critics may seem like a full-time job. Frankly, I don't think that one guy who decided to move from Cleveland to Miami to play basketball faced as much scrutiny. If you feel this way, trust me, you're not alone.

Before we dive into the chapter, let me ask you this: what are the initial thoughts that cloud your mind when you think of peer pressure? Smoking? Drinking? Drugs? You may be familiar with what peer pressure consists of but do you know what the phrase itself actually means? Let's take it apart and see what the words mean individually. The word peer is defined as an individual who has a lot in common with you including social class, income, abilities, etc. The word pressure, in this case, is someone or something that causes discomfort. In other words, peer pressure is something or someone who makes you feel uncomfortable in your own skin. Why is that, though? Are we so insecure to the point where we're not happy with ourselves? In order to be accepted by our peers, do we have to give in and follow orders or do we muster up the courage to refuse ditching our identities?

It all starts at a young age when you're at school or a playground and want to hang out with the popular kids. Remember those days? You want to gain the reputation as one of the "cool kids" by hanging out with a certain group of people. You dress a certain way, speak a certain way, and sometimes, walk a certain way to gain the attention of others. Why is it that we make these decisions, though? Could it be the feeling of accomplishment when we receive attention from certain people? Could it be the joy of "fitting in" perhaps driven by the fear of being an outcast? Whatever the case may be, many of us experience this and don't realize it until later in our lives, that it's better to be ourselves than to pretend to be someone else. We live in a world where we are judged by pretty much everything. We have to wear a certain brand of clothes, carry certain types of phones, and drive certain types of cars. Unfortunately, many of us give in to these trends and catch ourselves following the "in" crowd at some point in our lives.

While I've heard many people say that high school is the best four years of someone's life, I'm afraid I cannot attest to that. Personally, I thought high school was the worst four years of my life. It was more of a learning experience and a stepping-stone into the real world rather than enjoying it the way my friends did. For starters, I inherited responsibilities at a young age. My father was forced to undergo an open-heart surgery when I was just twelve years of age. The moment I heard that my father was going to go through surgery, I knew my life had changed forever. In order to make ends meet, I worked for a large corporate company and they sold pretty much everything including but not limited to electronics, clothing, appliances, lawn and garden products just to name a few.

High school was a time when I associated myself with the wrong type of people and experienced constant drama. They spread false rumors and made all types of accusations about me at school. Before I knew it, I had a bad reputation, even though I didn't deserve it. I can thank them for making my life a living hell. I had a few friends at school but we didn't really spend time with one another outside of school; I'm not sure why. As a result, I experienced high levels of depression. In the past, I used to constantly doubt myself and wasn't able to maintain a high self-esteem. I spent a lot of time wondering what people thought of me and why they spread the rumors that they did. In other words, I emotionally ate myself alive. I didn't know what to do with myself.

At some point, however, I realized that this was all in my head and decided that it was time for a change. I had become a prisoner of my insecurity and I couldn't continue to live this way. I started making gradual improvements on increasing my confidence and learned that I shouldn't pay attention to what my peers thought of me. After all, it's my life and I should live it the way I want to, not how others tell me to.

I strongly believe that every single individual living on this planet is here for a reason. That's what makes us unique and sets us apart from one another. We're here to make a difference and make our presence felt. How do we accomplish this? By introducing great innovations to the world; innovations we can benefit from for years. Speaking of great innovations, there are many of them that we use today such as the telephone, electricity, airplanes, automobiles, and many others. What if the people who invented these products decided to not invent them at all? They were all criticized by their peers; they were said to be crazy and out of their mind. Just think about it: What if Alexander Graham Bell, Benjamin Franklin, the Wright brothers, and Karl Benz gave in to criticism and allowed others to influence the decisions they made throughout their lives? What if they decided to follow the "in" crowd instead of standing their ground and leading the way? Would we still be using their products? Probably not.

    You may not be aware of this but there are many people out there who feel pressured into going out every weekend. Don't believe me? Just search the Internet. Many people go to the Internet for moral support when they feel guilty about not going out on a Friday or Saturday night. You know what? That's alright. There are some days where you're not in the mood to go out and you just want to be lazy and enjoy the comfort of our own home. One thing I've realized is that you save a lot of money when you don't go out. A night out on the town can cost a pretty penny, as well as a few extra calories. The great thing about staying home, sometimes, is that it allows you to find yourself. You realize that there are some things you've been meaning to do or catch-up on. It's never a bad idea to invite a friend or two and watch a movie together.

Society has found a way to put us on a guilt trip if we don't go out during the weekend. It makes us feel as though we are anti-social and completely disconnected from the rest of the world. FYI, it's all in your mind. More often than not, we convince ourselves into believing things that are not true. It's almost as if there's a little voice in the back of our heads telling us what to do. You're better off pressing the mute button when you hear that voice talking.

What are some of the negative issues when you choose to go out and party? Let's think about this for a second. Sometimes, we take our safety for granted. One of the things you have to worry about when going out is what might happen if things get rowdy and chaotic. On the bright side, you don't have to worry about that when you stay home every now and then. Things can get pretty crazy in a room filled with a lot of people especially when alcohol is present. Fights are no strangers to the bar and club scene. I think it's safe to say that almost all of us have either been in one or saved someone from getting into one. Therefore, don't feel bad when you decide to stay home on that Friday night. Chances are, you saved yourself from being hit by a beer bottle aimed at the person behind you.

Ever heard of "wrong place, wrong time?" Yeah, take that for kicks. When you're in the wrong place at the wrong time, things happen. Take my friend for instance. He was getting ready to graduate from high school and transfer to a four-year college with a full scholarship into their football program. He was definitely gifted and one of the most talented football players I had ever seen. Anyways, he had gone to his best friend's birthday party and alcohol was being served. It wasn't already bad enough that he was an underage drinker but he consumed enough alcohol to cause his body to blackout. He collapsed and apparently, someone had called 9-1-1 and next thing you know, he was in the ambulance fighting for his life. Unfortunately, he didn't make it. He passed away from the poisoning of his young liver and his brain. I was not there to witness this myself but I was devastated when I heard about it.

I wonder if his friends pressured him into drinking or did he want to drink in order to impress a certain someone or a certain group of people? Did someone push him into drinking that one last cup of alcohol before his body gave up on him? If that was the case, that one cup could've been the difference between life and death. All of these assumptions are valid since we'll never find out what really happened at the party.

Friends, or our peers, are supposed to help us make decisions that are in our best interest, not harm us. Not to say that our friends intentionally convince us into making bad decisions but things can go downhill fast, real fast. This goes to show that partying isn't what it's cracked up to be. People get hit, injured, or even killed just by being there. I'm not attempting to convince you to not go out and enjoy yourself but to be really careful of your surroundings. You can still have a great time without drinking but in case you do drink, make sure you're not driving and have a designated driver. After all, we [young adults] have a life ahead of us and have a long list of things to experience. Don't let someone else's decision be your last.

    Our parents are always trying to help us make better decisions in our lives. After all, they were our age at some point in their lives and underwent similar experiences as we are going through today. However, could that be the reason why we don't allow them to give us advice? Often, we believe that our parents don't understand the problems we face just because they are not our age and we end up pushing them away. Our parents experienced many of the same problems we face today. History is constantly repeating itself and growing pains are no exception. Personally, I enjoy feeling independent and having my privacy. I hardly tell my parents where I'm going or who I'm hanging out with. Is that the right thing to do, though? I mean, they are our parents and have watched us grow since day one. Is it fair that we block them out of our lives when they've been with us since day one? Call me crazy but I think a lot of it has to do with trust. We want to gain our parents' trust in order for them to know that we are making the right decisions. It's almost as if we want our parents to know that we are old enough to make our own decisions but yet, we don't know how to express it. Or maybe, we feel insulted when our parents ask us questions causing us to doubt the impression of ourselves we have placed before them.

What I would recommend is to sit down with your parents and explain how you feel. Let them know that expressing yourself can be tough sometimes and even though they may already know it, they will be glad to hear it from you. It may seem as though we hate them when we verbally push them away with our angry remarks but at the end of the day, we just want to make our parents proud.

In the "History" chapter of Emerson's Self-Reliance book, one of the points he made was that nothing exists in your life until you have tried it for yourself. A world outside of your home does not exist unless you walk outside and witness it. What is he exactly trying to say here? From what I understood, he is encouraging his readers to enjoy their lives and get a little taste of everything they desire. There are so many ways to have fun and be productive; the possibilities are endless. Make sure you don't live with any regrets. Keep in mind that Emerson's book was written in 1841, which means that his principles are still relevant today.

How does this tie in with peer pressure? There are many people out there, including myself, who prevent themselves from living life to the fullest. By doing so, they're setting barriers for themselves and mental obstacles to overcome. Is it really worth isolating yourself just because you're worried about what people are going to say or think of you? I came out of my shell when I was about twenty years old. I used to be timid and reserved but then I realized that I had only one life to live. I made a decision to put myself out there and never look back; I couldn't be any happier now.

No doubt, it's tough living in a world where you're always feeling as though you have to prove yourself to others. It's a never-ending process and an uphill battle unless you decide to make a change for the good. No one should be living their life where they feel like they have a chip on their shoulder. It might not seem as the ideal decision at the moment but convincing yourself to not allow others to have an influence on your decisions is a step in the right direction. Regardless of where you go and what you do, you're always going to receive criticism. That's why it's so important to maintain a high self-esteem at all times. It's a must to have complete confidence in what you do and the decisions you make. The key ingredient to success is to believe in yourself. In order to believe in yourself, you have to find yourself and it definitely doesn't start when you're too busy being someone else. If your peers don't allow you to be yourself and respect your decisions, then I say it's time you find yourself a new group of friends that are worthy of your time.

There are two things you must avoid in life: regrets and insecurities. If you have goals you want to accomplish, don't let anyone get in your way and stop you. Don't allow anyone to get in your head and get in the way of chasing your dreams. If you do, you will regret it for the rest of your life. Don't allow anyone to take control of you whether it's at a party or at school. You'd be surprised to hear the things people would say just to pick your brain. Remember, always be yourself and don't change for anyone. Appreciate what you have, both physically and mentally. There are many people in the world who are far less fortunate than you are and would do anything to be in your shoes. As a result, if you don't stay true to yourself, who would fill your shoes?

3
Food For Thought

When you're a college student, you may not make the healthiest decisions. Coffee becomes your best friend and sleep becomes your worst enemy. All you care about is studying for a test or typing that term paper due tomorrow. You could've typed that essay long before it was due but you decided to prepare it the night before. What's the word I'm looking for here? Oh yeah, procrastinate! Sorry, it's been a long day, as I didn't get any sleep last night. But I know what it's like because I've been there.

However, it doesn't end there. Don't forget about that big party this weekend. There's going to be a lot of alcohol there. Often, we give in to our temptations and don't have any remorse on our bodies. It's true, you are what you eat but what about the mind? As a college student, you endure so much stress whether it's related to finance, school, or even that relationship with your significant other. All of this can take a toll on your body. Even though we take a lot of things for granted, is this all a part of growing up? Do we use the trial and error method to find our strengths and weaknesses? If we are able to find ourselves, how do we embrace it? Although I'm not here to double as your health instructor, you're going to learn how to take care of your most valuable asset: your body.

Some of you may think that I sound a bit "old school" here but remember how people used to eat? They had to hunt for food. They were in better shape than we are today. They got the exercise they needed by hunting for animals and gained the nutrients their bodies needed. Sure, some of the food they ate might've been unsanitary but who's to say that the preservatives found in foods today are so much better? Preservatives are used to keep food from spoiling. Since the foods we buy today are transported throughout the country, they will rot without these preservatives. My point is that when you compare the food today to the food people used to eat tens and thousands of years ago, they were much healthier than some of the foods we eat today. Why? It's simple. They were natural. You might argue that some of the food people ate during those times carried diseases. While I'm not going to disagree with you, I'm going to ask you this: What if those foods were better prepared in order to get rid of any potential diseases? What if they didn't have preservatives and weren't frozen? When food is frozen, it loses the nutrients our bodies need and defeats the purpose of eating it. By eating, we are supposed to provide our bodies with the nutrients they need but what's happening when we are eating food without any nutrients? The term for that is "empty calories." What that means is you're consuming calories but not providing your body with any nutrients. Considering the foods found at super markets today, if you are able to find a healthy food item without any preservatives and reasonable nutrition facts, you might just be in luck.

    Over the years, it seems as though the variety of healthy food choices have decreased and the number of unhealthy foods we consume have increased. As we get older, we have more responsibilities. A lot of people depend on food to comfort them when they're stressed out or when they're having a bad day.

Not until recently was it that companies started labeling the nutrition facts on their products. However, this wasn't done because they woke up one morning and decided to do it for our benefit, the consumers. The truth of the matter is that they were actually being sued for selling unhealthy foods and were accused of causing obesity in our country. As a result, they started offering healthier choices such as salads, wraps, and so forth. However, just how healthy are these foods? Are they still considered healthy after you add your favorite toppings such as cheese, ranch dressing, etc.? They might be healthier compared to the other items on their menus but just how healthy can frozen food be?

Companies have learned that we, the consumers, want to eat healthy. That could be the reason why we've been seeing products that include the words diet, sugar–free, no sugar added, etc. However, does a can of soda become healthy all of a sudden just by writing diet all over it? I think you know where I'm going with this. In my opinion, it does not. Diet soda contains artificial sweeteners, or "fake sugar." If that wasn't bad enough, you have to worry about the acids that are found in soda. In other words, diet soda is not a healthy choice especially if you're trying to lose weight.

Let's use another example: This time, let's talk about the salads found at fast food burger joints. In order to keep you sane and prevent you from honking your horn like a mad man because you lost count of how long you've been waiting at the drive-thru window, most fast food restaurants have to use frozen foods. They can't cook it while you're waiting in the drive-thru along with other customers waiting for their orders. It would just take too long to make them from scratch.

You might want to know if a salad from a fast food restaurant is healthy. It all depends on where you go and how the salad is prepared. Also, the toppings and dressings, if any, play a huge role in the calorie count. One of the worst things you can do is to ask for ranch dressing on your salad. Yes, it tastes awesome and makes a salad less painful to eat but what's the point of eating an unhealthy salad? You might as well be eating the burger and fries you convinced yourself not to eat. Since this isn't a guide to eating healthy, I will have to stop here and refrain myself from going overboard. If you have access to the Internet, you can look up tons of articles and websites that have a list of healthy food choices that are low on calories, sugar, sodium, carbs, the whole nine.

Being a business student, I was never a fan of science. However, there's an exception to everything, as I had a lot of fun learning things I wasn't aware of in my Anthropology class. I had an amazing professor who genuinely cared for the well-being and success of her students. She introduced a lot of new concepts and exposed us to a completely different world. One of the things I learned was that the USDA doesn't have the time to check every single food item found at your local grocery store. Even if they tried to, there's just not enough time to check everything. They inspect only a small portion of the foods that we eventually put in our bodies. Interested in finding out how it works? The USDA will only take a look at a product when there have been multiple reports of the health issues a certain food product may have caused. So, this raises a good question: We are seeing a lot of new products on the market but are they safe? Will they have a short-term or long-term impact on our health? Who knows? This leads us to my next point.

One of the other things I learned in my Anthropology class is that the food we consume will have an impact on our children's gene structure; it's been like that for years. There are a lot of companies out there who are taking advantage of our hectic and stressful lifestyles; they're putting a lot of emphasis on energy. They are well aware of the fact that we do not get enough sleep at night and need energy to get through the next day. As a result, energy drinks have become very popular. Now, while this may make the marketers and producers happy, are these products healthy? What sort of impact will they have on our bodies both short-term and long-term? Will they have an impact on our children and generations to come?

The problem with these products is that they're fairly new to the market and haven't been time-tested. As a result, we don't know what they're capable of. Looking at the nutrition facts of a regular energy drink, you will notice that it contains a lot of sugar. A single can might not cause you to become diabetic but what if you decide to drink more than one? What if you depend on these energy drinks to support your busy lifestyle? Let's go back to fundamentals: The consumption of excess amounts of sugar causes your body to prevent diabetes. As I mentioned earlier, we don't know much about these products. And since we don't know, is it safe to say that there's a high chance of being diagnosed with diabetes?

I had a hectic class schedule last semester and since I didn't get much sleep a few days before the final exams, I had a few energy drinks. Yes, they did help but it was only temporary. Whenever I had more than one, my body reacted in a funny way and I have to admit, it was scary at one point. That's when I realized the damage I was causing to my body. I could feel as if I were "bouncing off the walls" and I got jittery. As a result, I stopped drinking those energy drinks because it just wasn't worth putting my health in jeopardy.

These companies who specialize in manufacturing energy products spend a lot of money advertising their products. They have been able to tap into the world of action sports and become sponsors. It's not just an energy product anymore, it's a lifestyle. Some of your favorite athletes might be sponsored by one of these companies. They are trying to convince as many people as they can to buy their products, just like every other business. However, since these products are new to the market, would that make us the guinea pigs so to speak? After all, we are the first generation to try out these products and if they have negative side effects, future generations might have to suffer from the consequences.

Speaking of a stressful lifestyle, we all experience stress at some point in our lives. After all, we're all humans and we can only take so much. Believe it or not but recent studies show that stress is one of the leading causes of death along with smoking and obesity. When we experience stress, how do we deal with it? Some people depend on smoking, alcohol, and/or resort to drugs. I'm not here to tell you why smoking, drinking alcohol, and doing drugs is bad for you; I'm pretty sure you're already aware of that. Instead, I'm going to give you a few tips on how you can deal with stress.

Stress enters and leaves our bodies every so often. If you were to depend on smoking, drinking, or even drugs, how would your body react to that? By consuming any of those three, you would cause severe damage to your body. You would think that you're escaping your problems and getting rid of stress by either smoking, drinking, doing drugs, or maybe even all three but in reality, you're just damaging your body. After it's all said and done, your problems are still there but the long-term damage you have brought upon yourself is there to stay. By resorting to bad habits, you're taking advantage of what they have to offer and that's to take you to a world where none of your problems exist. This is only temporary, not permanent. You're actually putting yourself in a worse position than you were before and taking several steps back by resorting to these bad habits. After the feeling is gone, you're still going to have deal with the same problems you tried to run away from earlier. So, what's the purpose of harming your body? What are the long-term consequences?

Here are a few ways you can deal with stress without harming your body. What's something you really enjoy doing? For example, I really enjoy going to the gym, playing basketball, and listening to music. Let's say I come home from a bad day at work. I didn't meet my goals for the day and my manager is threatening to fire me. Usually, I would be depressed and because of this, hypothetically speaking of course, I would have to smoke a cigarette and pop the cap off of a cold one. That's not something I should be doing. Instead, I can call a few friends and see if they would want to play a game of basketball at the local park. This way, I can take my mind off from work and get myself out of the house. Usually, it helps me a lot when I'm stressed out and go outdoors. I don't feel isolated and getting some fresh air doesn't hurt either.

Let's change the scenario a little bit. Let's say you want to play basketball but your friends aren't available. That's fine, no worries. You can always go to the gym to lift some weights or run on the treadmill and take your anger out on that. This is definitely a lot better than smoking and drinking. This way, you're not only dealing with stress but you're staying in shape as well. A few other things you can do are listen to music, walk at the park, or even go for a drive. It allows you to cool down and collect your thoughts. It always helps to call a friend and hear what they have to say. It's comforting to hear someone else's perspective on a certain situation. Do everything in your power to stay away from the consumption of tobacco, alcohol, or any type of drug that is a threat to your health.

I promised you that I was going to write about the aspects of life that ambush your mind and emotions. Before we dive deeper into this topic, let's figure out some of the roadblocks that get in our way. WARNING: Please don't print out a picture of my face and throw darts at it if I don't list the situation you're experiencing at the moment.

First, education. Need I say more? It's the key to success. You can't live with it, you can't live without it. Let's face it. We've all found ourselves questioning whether or not school is right for us. Why do we think that way? Going to school can be stressful especially when you don't understand what's being taught in the classroom. There are many assignments and due dates to keep track of. If you're like me, you don't jot down any due dates. You just keep repeating it to yourself until you get tired of it and get to work. In most cases, it's not until the night before it's due. For some reason, I thrive under pressure. I feel the adrenaline rush and put the pedal to the metal. Oh yeah, we can't forget about those tests and exams. What would we do without them? We study as hard as we can only to find out we didn't do as well as we expected. What happens when you pass an exam by just a few points? Do you put in the same effort for the next test? Assuming you actually put in the time to study the material, do you spend more time preparing for the next one?

This is something I can relate to. I was never a "straight A" student. I always struggled with most subjects, especially with math. I excelled when it came to writing essays but math wasn't my thing. Now, does this mean I'm retarded? Does this mean that I have learning disabilities? Does this mean that I should drop out of school just because the other students in the class are getting better grades than I am? And what about the students with ADHD, dyslexia, or any other learning disability? How should they feel? What should they do if they're not receiving the attention they need? Should they drop out as well?

Next, relationships. Now, the term relationship is used loosely. You can have a relationship with a friend, a parent, a relative, or an intimate partner. Emotions come in all shape and sizes. Such emotions would include feeling content, upset, angry, and so forth. Since happiness doesn't have as many side effects as anger and sadness, let's focus on those two. Not everyone has a family. Not everyone knows who their parents are. Not everyone has an intimate partner. They say you don't realize what you have until it's gone, but what if you don't have it to begin with? Do you take people for granted? Or does anyone take you for granted?

You've experienced various types of relationships. People always come and go, as it's a part of life. But what happens when the people who are closest to you let you down? What if you can't trust them anymore? Would you be able to look at them the same way? Would you accept their apology?

Being a college student and a young adult, you know a lot of people. You categorize these people into different groups. You have friends that you get in touch with when you want to see a movie. You have a certain group of friends that you like to party with. However, we have "all-purpose" friends. These friends aren't just any friends. They're friends that we can call or text any time of the day and they are up for anything. I guess you can consider them as your "road dogs." Day in and day out, you depend on these "all-purpose" friends and expect them to be there when you need them the most. They are closer to you than your other friends. But what happens when something goes wrong? Let's take a look.

Here, I'm going to create two fictional characters and use them as an example. Randy and Zach have been best friends as long as they can remember. They were childhood friends and attended the same schools together. They have a lot in common and share a lot of memories. They had a great friendship and everything was great until one day, Zach decided to backstab Randy. Since there are so many possibilities, I'm going to let you choose what happened and why Zach did what he did. Later, Randy finds out what happened and is upset with Zach. He feels betrayed and helpless. Zach was the only person that Randy trusted. Randy was a reserved individual and didn't open up to just anyone. It took a lot for Randy to reveal his emotions and deep thoughts. As a result, this was a hard pill for Randy to swallow. He took this very seriously and somewhat blamed himself for the incident.

The reason why I didn't specify the incident that took place is because all of us have experienced the feeling of betrayal from the people we love the most but not everyone experiences the same scenario. Unfortunately, it's not just with friends. Many people such as our parents or boyfriends and girlfriends do things that hurt us. Sometimes, it's not intentional but it happens. Many of us have parents that love us unconditionally. But what about the children who live in foster homes due to their parents' decision to not be a part of their lives? What about the people who have never been in an intimate relationship and their knowledge of one is based on the stretch of their imagination? What are these people supposed to do?

Last but not least, money. When you're a young adult and a college student, money comes in and goes sooner than you know it. If a genie was to grant you three wishes, I'm sure all three wishes would translate to dollars. If only we can get an unlimited supply of it, wouldn't that be great? Since money doesn't grow on trees, we have to keep an eye on where our hard earned money goes. But what happens when we allow money to get the best of us? What happens when we can't afford the finer things in life?

For example, I've always wanted to own a muscle car. Ever since I was a kid, I would dream of driving one every day with the biggest smile on my face. I love the way they sound. As a matter of fact, it's music to my ears. Newsflash, I have yet to own a muscle car. But what am I supposed to do? How am I supposed to feel? Am I supposed to beat myself over it and feel depressed? Am I supposed to sit in a corner and cry? Obviously not. Hey, I have to pay my bills every month. I'm sure I will come to a point in my life when I will be able to afford one and live my dreams but that doesn't mean I'm supposed to place myself in an emotional coma and hide in a cave.

As young adults and college students, our desires are deeper than our pockets. There are a lot of things we want but cannot afford. It's very important to prioritize your finances. For example, if you have your own place, then you have to worry about rent, utilities, etc. These obligations come first unless you want to get evacuated or sit in the dark. You can't convince yourself that you will magically come up with the money to pay for your rent the day before it's due. It just doesn't work that way. It would've been nice if it did, though.

If you're known to be a window shopper, there are alternatives you can look into. Need a new pair of jeans? There are many stores where you can find clothing at a discounted price. Now, they might not be the latest fashion but consider the money you would be saving. Here's a good example: Let's say your favorite designer jeans cost about $80 before tax. And that's just one pair. The smart thing to do is to shop for less expensive alternatives. Better yet, turn around and pretend that you never saw those jeans. Okay, so now you find yourself trying on a few pairs of jeans that cost about $30 before tax. You can buy two pairs of jeans, and maybe a shirt or two to create two different outfits. That's a lot better than paying $80 just for a single pair of jeans. And oh, that doesn't include a top.

Not everyone is going to entertain the idea of whether or not they should purchase a pair of jeans for $80. Just like I want to own a muscle car, you're going to want to purchase what you desire. The possibilities are endless. The rule of thumb is to live within your means, not beyond. If you can't afford something, so what? It's not the end of the world. Opportunities will always present themselves. You might not be able to afford it at the moment but you might be able to at some point down the road.

Never feel guilty about rewarding yourself. Work hard, play hard. It's always a good idea to compromise, though. Don't forget to buy the things you need while setting some money aside and saving it for a rainy day. Be sure to separate your wants and needs. If you have some money left over after paying the bills, then you're in great position. However, if you had to borrow $80 from Danny next door to pay your phone bill, then you're probably better off waiting until your next paycheck.

As you can see, many young adults and college students face many mental obstacles each and every day. Our patience and our intelligence are tested. What are you supposed to do if push comes to shove and the going gets tough? Feeling discouraged, you lose every ounce of hope. How do you get back up and stand on your own two feet? Does it include the consumption of alcohol and/or tobacco? I've noticed that many young adults and college students turn to alcohol and tobacco when they find themselves in what I like to call a "mental ditch". You might be asking yourself, "What is this 'mental ditch' he's speaking of?" A mental ditch is when you feel like you're trapped and don't have anywhere to go, mentally of course. You don't see the light at the end of the tunnel and live in complete darkness. In other words, you lose hope and confidence in yourself.

I can't tell you what decisions to make nor how to live your life. However, I can tell you one thing: Alcohol and tobacco are NOT the answer to your problems; they just add insult to injury. They might be a temporary fix and eliminate stress for the time being, but they're doing more harm than good. What's the best way to put it? There is none really. They damage your body and the worst part is, you don't feel it until you get older. How's that a bad thing? Let's say you have bad drinking and smoking habits. You're telling yourself that you feel fine, you don't have any health issues and this results in more consumption of alcohol and tobacco. More consumption, more health problems when you get older. It's that simple.

Whether you're a young adult or a parent, you're going to want to stay healthy. If you're a young adult, you have a whole life ahead of you and have a lot of memories to create; you don't want to miss out on them. If you're an adult, especially a parent, then you must stay healthy by all means necessary. Perhaps, you have children that depend on you and the last thing you want to do is put yourself in a position where you won't able to support them.

Regardless of age, staying healthy and in shape is key. If you're serious about staying healthy, develop a plan and stick to it. It should include a diet and an exercise routine. Worried about staying on track? You can find a workout buddy who is willing to participate and you can motivate one another. Unlike video games, there's no cheat code that allows you to restore your health.

Although being healthy and staying in shape requires physical exercise and a balanced diet, it doesn't end there. Being healthy also means that you have a clear conscience and appreciate what you have. That way, you're not always stressed out about what you don't have. I promise you that it will pay off. Remember, there are a lot of people who are far less fortunate than you. While you're hoping your parents would buy you the latest smartphone, there are many people who don't have a cell phone, period. They can't call their parents and let them know they're on their way home from school. While you're picturing yourself wearing the trendiest pair of designer jeans to impress your friends, there are many people who don't even have a pair of jeans to protect themselves from harsh weather conditions and wild infestation,

Adopting a pessimistic state of mind will only drag you down. Reminding yourself to remain optimistic, regardless of the situation, will take you a long way. Make sure you take care of your body, both emotionally and physically; it will take care of you. With so many people taking their health for granted, they're suffering the consequences. There are a lot of people out there who commit suicide just because they're not happy with themselves or what they have. Also, there are people who depend on anti-depression pills in order to keep sane. Please, take initiative of your well-being and do everything in your power to avoid becoming another statistic.

4
Swipe Responsibly

Credit is arguably one of the greatest tools in today's world. It allows us to buy or rent a house or an apartment, and finance many of the things we need and depend on daily such as appliances, furniture, and big screen televisions that we can show off when our friends come over to watch the big game. Alright, maybe we don't need a big screen television but it's always nice to have bragging rights as being the neighbor with the biggest television on the block. When faced with any situation where we need to borrow money, having good credit can be a lifesaver. It can be the difference between having a car or relying on public transportation. It can also be the difference between moving out or living with your parents. Don't get me wrong, living with your parents has its own perks but that's besides the point here. We live in a world where materialistic items are a hot commodity and what happens when we can't afford them? Do we execute desperate measures during desperate times? In a world where cash used to be king, has it been thrown off of its throne by credit cards as the new kid on the block? Stay tuned to find out.

Here's a little-known fact of the day for most of you: The credit system is only a few hundred years old. It can be traced back to retail stores who sold big-ticket items such as electronics, appliances, and furniture. These retail stores noticed that the average consumer wasn't able to afford these items. By extending credit to their customers, it allowed their customers to purchase the items they needed and essentially, it increased their sales revenue.

What does the credit system have in common now and when it originally started? One word, convenience. I'm sure you've seen those credit card commercials where people are buying food at a cafeteria and everyone is paying with their credit cards. All of a sudden, someone decides to write a check and it leads to complete chaos. Obviously, you're not going to see that in real life but you will occasionally see someone writing a check. The whole point of those commercials is to demonstrate the convenience of a credit card. It's quick, fast, and easy to use. Unlike cash, you don't have to worry about it if it gets lost or stolen. It just takes one phone call to report it as lost or stolen. However, is that the downfall? Is it too convenient and too easy for us to use to the point where it's more harmful than beneficial?

Not using a credit card responsibly can have serious side effects. I can totally see this as a commercial, similar to alcohol commercials where they advise you to drink responsibly, or those 30-second drug commercials where they explain the benefits of the drug for 28 seconds and squeeze in the side effects at the last 2 seconds of the commercial so you wouldn't be able to understand anything.

Back to the matter at hand, do we blame credit cards for putting us in debt or do we take responsibility of our own actions? This is kind of like saying I gained weight from eating too much fast food and it's their fault for making such great tasting food. But see, that's the thing. That's what banks want you to do. They want you to keep charging your credit cards and make minimum payments. Those minimum payments don't help you pay off the balance because you're almost paying a month's worth of interest charges. I mean, you can't blame them because they're in business and no one runs a business without having the intent to generate profit. You know what's funny? They hope and wish you would pay them back instead of defaulting on your credit cards.

Having a credit card can be a blessing and a curse to some people, sort of like having super powers. They're not useful unless you use them to fight against evil. Not sure why I'm telling you this or better yet, why did I think of this? Whatever you do, don't ask. Anyways, using a credit card should be taken seriously. If you find yourself not being able to pay the minimum payment for a month or two, it could quickly go downhill from there. I don't want that to happen to you, though. Later in this chapter, you will come across some information that will benefit you and hopefully, allow you to make more informed decisions in terms of credit related matters.

Before we begin, I want you to think about how you spend your money. Where does it come from? Do you use cash or a debit/credit card to pay for all of your purchases? If you're a college student, chances are that you receive financial aid. I'm not trying to say that financial aid is a bad thing. I can't tell you how many of my friends don't care how or where they get the money from as long as they can spend it. They too, receive financial aid. One thing I noticed is that unlike in the past, you have access to your financial funds on a debit card. In the past, you would have to wait to receive a check in the mail and you could either cash it or deposit the check straight into your checking account. Nowadays, with the increasing use of debit and credit cards, you receive your financial aid money on a debit card rather than a check. Need cash? You can go to an ATM and withdraw the cash you need. By having access to your funds on a debit card, it's a lot more convenient and easier than ever before. However, could this be a bad thing? Keep in mind that financial aid is a federal grant. A federal grant, unlike a loan, does not have to be repaid. Combine those two aspects together and what do you get? Money that you have easy access to and you don't have to worry about repaying it. Or simply put, a shopping spree. Is that a recipe for disaster? You tell me.

By allowing college students to spend financial aid funds on a debit card, does that discipline them on how to use a credit card? Here's a good analogy: When we were kids, we learned how to ride a bike with training wheels. We used training wheels to learn how to balance ourselves. So, could we use these pre-loaded debit cards to discipline ourselves and learn how to use credit cards? In theory? Yes. In practice? Not really. It doesn't always work out the way we want it to. However, if you have strong willpower, you have control. What I'm trying to say here is that if we can use these debit cards with our financial aid funds wisely, we can do the same thing with credit cards. Unlike financial aid, credit cards are considered as loans. What does that mean? They have to be repaid.

Unfortunately, much like the debit card that comes pre-loaded with our financial aid funds, many of us go on a shopping spree and use our credit cards to get everything we want. What's even more unfortunate is that we max out our credit cards without realizing the consequences. If there were a term to describe this action, it would probably be "reckless spending". But you can't blame yourself entirely when it happens to you. Because there's no exchange of actual money, you don't realize how much you're spending until the monthly statement comes in the mail.

The biggest problem, in my opinion, is that many young adults and college students alike are not familiar with how credit works. They find themselves charging their credit cards like no tomorrow without having any remorse on their checking accounts. They fool themselves into thinking that they will be able to pay it off someday and hope to keep making minimum payments in the mean time. They don't realize the value and importance of having good credit until it's time to buy a new house or finance a new car. At that point, it might be a little too late. However, it's never too late to start building credit. Neither is it too early to start learning about credit. Let me ask you this, though. Do we blame our parents for not teaching us the ropes to credit at an early age or do we blame society for creating a world where we are judged by our materialistic possessions? I strongly believe that both play a huge role in our lives. It's sort of like being in a boxing match. Would you want to constantly get punched in the face or do you want to fight back? Do you want to educate yourself on credit matters or do you want to make enough mistakes to regret having credit cards? Do you want to keep wasting money on things you don't need or do you want to buy what's important and set aside the money you saved?

Knowing the importance of credit, I applied for my first credit card as soon as I turned eighteen years old. I ran into a few online forums where they discussed the "ins" and "outs" of credit. I devoted a couple of hours a day to read the information posted by forum members. When I applied for my first credit card, I had a part-time job and luckily, I was approved for a credit card with a small spending limit. I was kind of disappointed by the fact that I was approved for a small limit but I knew I had to start somewhere and get on the training wheels. I used my card and made the payments religiously. After all, there's not much you can buy for $500, which was the original limit. About two months later, I got approved for another credit card and this time, I got approved for a higher credit limit. If I recall, the second credit card I got approved for had a spending limit of $800.

I got addicted to the great feeling of being approved. I got a little carried away and applied for a few more cards; I decided to stop applying for quite some time. I was under the mistaken impression that the more cards I had, the better my credit score (that number that gives you the "value" of your credit history) would be. It was not until later, long after I had stopped applying for more cards, that I learned it actually doesn't help at all. I was on my best behavior and was determined not to max out my credit cards. Right before I turned nineteen, I was able to buy a car with the help of my father who co-signed for me. I paid the down payment and it was a great feeling. My hard work finally paid off when I bought a car in my own name, without a co-signer, when I was just twenty-one years old. To this day, I'm proud of that accomplishment.

Just for the record, I'm not making any attempts to brag but rather encourage many others to do the same. Initially, it might be tough to hold back from using that shiny new credit card but it will be worth it when you use your good credit to sign on the dotted line with your name and your name only. If you use it, use it wisely, pay it off quickly, and plan for the long-term rather than the short-term and you will be successful.

I'm not going to get into the specifics here but there are a few things that I'm going to throw out there that I believe you will find very beneficial. First and foremost, many people believe that by having many credit cards and being able to manage them, they will strengthen their credit report. On the contrary, when a creditor, or a lender, looks at your credit report and sees multiple credit card accounts opened with a short period of time, they might not feel too comfortable about extending credit to you, thinking that you are too dependent on credit and financially unstable. This is something you would want to avoid at all costs.

Next, a common mistake people make is to use their credit cards either for many, various small purchases or buying big-ticket items to prove to their lenders that they are able to pay off their debt and are responsible enough to handle larger spending limits. However, this is not true because the more you use your credit cards, the more desperate you seem to your lender. Believe it or not but you can use your credit card for a single small purchase and still build great credit. For example, let's say you have a credit card with a $1,000 limit. You go to your local electronic store and buy a TV for $900 thinking that you are building credit by making a large purchase. You're planning to pay it off within the next three months but what if you're not able to pay it off within that time frame? What if you're not able to make minimum payments at all? These are some things you have to take into consideration.

Here's a different scenario: Let's say you use your credit card, the same one, to buy a cup of coffee instead of a new TV. You go home and make the payment right away so that you won't forget later. You know what? That's perfectly fine because the end result on your credit report is going to be the same. The key is to use your credit card at least once a month in order to keep it active and use it for a small purchase. You don't have to make large purchases to build good credit. Making small purchases and paying them off is just the same because when creditors look at your report, they're going to check the payment history and whether or not you've been making your payments on time. What's interesting is that even though creditors lend you money, they don't want you to spend it. When you have a credit card with a $1,000 limit and making small purchases, your creditor knows that they can trust you with a larger limit because you're not going to go on a shopping spree and buy things left and right. By making small purchases, you avoid paying interest and burying yourself in debt.

Finally, many people believe that their credit scores are impacted every time they don't get approved when they apply for a credit card or a loan. The truth is that if you apply for too many of them, it will have an impact on your credit score regardless of what the outcome is. Your credit score is not impacted by every single credit inquiry. A credit inquiry is simply used to describe the process of a lender inquiring, or checking, your credit report. Having too many inquiries causes a lender to believe that you are desperate and are trying to abuse any credit you can get your hands on. When this happens, you will have a really tough time obtaining credit. This is something you definitely want to avoid as well. I know I gave you a lot of information to absorb but you will learn as you go along. I highly recommend visiting and browsing a few online forums. Read and familiarize yourself with the terminology. You don't have to spend a whole day, just spend a an hour or two a day. Before you know it, you will be a pro.

When you walk into your local electronics, appliance, or hardware store, there's a good chance you will notice that they are advertising some type of interest offer when you use their store credit card. Usually, they will offer either no or low interest charges for a period of time. Here's what they don't want you to know: Let's say you buy a computer for $1,000 and finance it. The offer at the time of purchase is no interest for 12 months. So far so good. Now, you receive your statement a few weeks later and see a very minimum low payment and you say to yourself, "Hey, I can afford this!" So, you make minimum payments for 12 months thinking that the balance is going to be paid off before the interest kicks in, right? Wrong. If you don't pay off your entire balance within those twelve months, they will charge you interest from the day you bought that computer. Also, the interest rate isn't low either. Store credit cards usually carry an interest in the low to mid 20's. Want to avoid putting yourself in this situation? If you can afford to pay cash for the entire purchase instead of using your credit card, then go ahead and do so because you will have one less thing to worry about.

On the other hand, for someone who wants to start building credit, gas and store cards are the way to go; they are fairly easy to get approved for. Usually, credit cards offered through clothing stores and gas stations approve applicants who have little to no credit. If you're looking to build credit, that's something you should look into. You might be asking yourself, "What's a good number of credit cards to have?" According to the Fair Isaac scoring system, or FICO, you must have at least 2 credit cards. FICO is the scoring system creditors use when you apply for a loan. In addition to your income and credit history, they also look at your credit scores. I don't want to get into the specifics of the FICO scoring system because it will throw me off topic. However, you can look it up online and find a great deal of information. I highly recommend you do so.

I'm not sure what's the reasoning behind this but a lot of people believe that they can build credit with a debit card. Activity for debit cards, nor checking accounts, does NOT appear on your credit reports like credit cards and loans do. If you're a strong advocate of using a debit card, be my guest. There is nothing wrong with using a debit card because it allows you to spend within your means. It doesn't give you an opportunity to owe money to a lender because you're spending your own money, not theirs. What I would highly suggest is to take your credit card for a spin once a month and best of all, you don't have to go out of your way to use it. You can use it for purchases that you would normally use to pay with your debit card such as a tank of gas or a cup of coffee. After you've used your credit card, you can remove it from your wallet and place it somewhere you feel comfortable. This way, you don't have to worry about being tempted to use your credit card. A good idea is to have your credit card with you at all times and use it in case of an emergency. If you don't trust yourself with it, you can always place it in the back of your wallet or somewhere that you won't be able to a get hold of quickly but still have access to it.

Let's get to the good stuff now. Let's talk about something we all love and can't get enough of: If you guessed money, then you guessed right. You have to ask yourself, "Should I apply for a credit card if I don't have a job?" My answer to that is yes and no but let me tell you why. If you don't have a job, I highly recommend that you don't apply for a credit card. If you do apply, there's a really good chance that you are going to use that credit card for small purchases here and there. Those small purchases add up rather quickly and before you know it, you have incurred a pretty hefty balance. At that point, you will most likely convince yourself that you will eventually get a job and pay it off. However, if you have great willpower, I highly recommend that you get a credit card and use it for one purchase only. That purchase can be for a bottle of water, soda, coffee, or something under $5. That way, you can build credit even though you don't have a job. A rule of thumb is to start building credit at an early age. The sooner you start building, the better because you will have a long history of on-time payments and the longer your credit history, the better your chances are of getting approved for a car loan or an apartment you may need to lease or finance in the future. Building credit takes time and having excellent credit doesn't happen overnight.

If you're on a budget, here are two good tips: First, it's always a good idea to set some money aside from your usual income regardless of the source. If you have a job, you might want to save 10% of your paycheck and establish an emergency fund. An emergency fund doesn't have to be formal. It can be a savings account at a financial institution or cash under your mattress. The whole point of having an emergency fund is to give yourself some cushion. It allows you to save up some money and use it on a rainy day. I mean, expenses never end and sometimes, they rise to the occasion when you least expect them to. Also, if you're in the market for a new car, it's always a good idea to go the used car route. When it comes to used cars, I highly recommend searching for a used car from a Japanese manufacturer because they are known to be reliable and having lower cost of ownership compared to other car manufacturers. Not to say that cars from other manufacturers are not reliable but generally, you can never go wrong with a used car from a Japanese manufacturer.

To wrap this up, I can't tell you how important credit is. Honestly, I would say it's right up there with your health and college degree. Without having good credit, it's going to be difficult buying pricey items or financing a house or an apartment. Since the majority of us cannot afford to write a check for $200,000, we are dependent on our credit. I strongly believe that some people take credit for granted and think of it as a right rather than a privilege. Never underestimate the value of our credit system and it's always a good idea to get a head start on the building process. Come to think of it, it's very similar to your résumé. The longer your work experience, the more you're likely to find a job due to the manager feeling comfortable hiring a new employee who has a long history of work experience.

The same thing goes for credit; the longer your credit history, the better your chances are of getting approved for a loan. Frankly, you want to have a positive credit history, not negative. Many of you may not be aware of this but there are employers out there who check your credit reports and partially base their decision on your credit history. I remember reading a few articles where employees of various companies were not promoted due to a poor credit history. They were notified that they wouldn't be promoted until they cleaned up their credit reports and increased their credit scores. It seems as though your credit is just as important as your work experience and criminal background, depending on the position you're applying for.

Again, there is an abundance of information for you to learn online and the best part is that it's free. All you need to do is devote some time and read the information posted by forum members. That's how I learned how to build my credit and I am really thankful for that, as it changed my life. If it changed my life, it can change yours too. I know I gave you a lot of information to learn but once you get an understanding of how everything works, you'll be glad you took a step in the right direction and you can benefit from it for the rest of your life.

5
Dollars and Sense

When it comes to attending college, many students are privileged. They can continue to live with their parents and rely on their support while they work towards their degree. They may even have the luxury of not needing a job at all, but simply focusing on school only. However, others do not live that way. They are forced to earn a living while going to school just to keep the lights on and put food on the table. Depending on the circumstances, students who move out and find a new place to call home have to support themselves financially. As for the students who live with their family members, either they are fortunate enough to have financial support from other members living in the same household or they have to support everyone else in the household. It can go either way. The students who juggle a lifestyle of working and learning may feel that they're at a disadvantage. However, is it really a disadvantage? Would it be beneficial for someone to gain work experience as they pursue an educational degree rather than just focus on attending school? We will take a look into this later in the chapter.

As a first-generation college student from a working-class family, I never imagined that someday I would be able to say that I was attending school to earn an academic degree. As I mentioned in the second chapter, I started working at a young age and haven't stopped since. My parents always taught me the sky's the limit as long as I worked hard. After I graduated from high school, I went straight to work. I entertained the idea of attending a local community college but instead, I directed all of my focus and attention to making a living. At the time, I strongly believed in success within the working world… choose a career path and grow within a company. I didn't take my first college class until I was twenty-one years of age.

With competition in the job market becoming tougher by the day, I decided to work towards an academic degree. Also, I wanted to meet new people and make some important connections. At a local community college, I registered for entry-level English and Math courses. After I finished the semester, I made up my mind that I wanted to continue with my education and become a full-time student, majoring in Business Management. I wanted to graduate and earn my degree in the shortest amount of time. However, all that changed when my family needed my financial support so I dropped out of college and began working two part-time jobs.

In order to come home with a bigger paycheck, I decided to become a car salesman since it was a commission-based position. I've always been a really good salesman and wanted to take advantage of it. I was counting on the fact that I would have a big paycheck by selling a lot of cars. Long story short, I didn't enjoy it at all. I worked six days a week and long hours just to hit my sales goals. There was no job security and no consistent, stable income. It got to a point where I decided to make a change. I always felt stressed from work and didn't really have time for a social life. Most of my time was devoted to work and I wanted to relax on my spare time. That's when I decided to go back to school. I knew I couldn't continue living my life this way and wanted something better. As a result, I enrolled into a local community college. My first semester there, I took 17 units while working part-time as a bank teller. It was really tough balancing work and school. There were many long days when I would come home worn out and exhausted; all I wanted to do was sleep. Instead, I had to complete the homework due the next day.

After I finished the semester, I decided to resign from my teller position in order to become a full-time student. This time, there was no sudden family crisis… everything went as planned; I didn't have to drop out of college again. Not too many people were supportive of my decision to take 32 units in the coming semester. Yes, you read that right: 32 units! My friends and relatives told me that I wasn't going to be able to get through the whole semester without dropping any classes. But I must admit that I was driven. Sure enough, the semester ended and I was done with 32 units.

In case you're wondering what classes I took, they included Law 1 (Business Law), Statistics 1, Accounting 1, Spanish 2, English 1A (Freshman Composition), CSIT 401 (an entry-level computer class required for my major), Music 21 (Music Appreciation), Economics 1, and Anthropology 101. I attended three different community colleges, six days a week. Kids, please don't try this at home. I wouldn't recommend doing this because it was a struggle.

Even though I wasn't working at the time, I still had to stay up late to get all the work done. The first half of the semester wasn't as demanding as the second half due to the term papers and final exams. I had to make a lot of sacrifices but I was the happiest man on the planet when it was all said and done. It almost felt like going to war and coming back unharmed. I can tell you that a lot of people were shocked when they found out that I got through the semester all in one piece and congratulated me on my major accomplishment.

You might be convinced that I was officially out of my mind. Maybe I was. The reason why I took so many classes in such a short period of time was to make up for the time I didn't go to school. I wanted to catch up to where I thought I should've been so I could graduate "on-time". After crunching some numbers, I figured that if I had started taking classes and worked part-time after graduating from high school, I would've graduated by the age of twenty-two or twenty-three. Thanks to my hard work, I will be graduating soon and transferring to a four-year college at the age of twenty-three.

How did I survive without having a source of income you ask? Luckily, I saved money by transferring money every time I received my paycheck while I was working. Even though I couldn't see myself quitting work completely if I retuned to school, things just worked out that way.

I'm glad I brought this up because I wanted to talk to you about the importance of saving money. Gosh, I sound like my mother right now. Saving money may seem like a naïve thing to do but honestly, you will be glad you did. When you need money and don't have it, you will feel as though you are trapped in a room where all four walls are closing on you every second. You don't want to experience that feeling. Trust me; it's not fun to say the least. I know I talked about this in the previous chapter but I want to talk about it again. It's that important!

If you're like me and many other hard-working Americans, there aren't many options available when you're stuck in a ditch. Unless you have a wealthy relative you didn't know about or an inheritance waiting for you, most of your options, if not all, are somehow connected to a creditor who is willing to lend money at a price. Creditors usually charge an insane interest rate when providing you with a loan. As if it that wasn't bad enough, you have to worry about making payments and that's going to be really tough if you're not working at the moment. Much like student loans, many creditors who tell you that you don't need to make payments for a certain period of time charge an arm and a leg in interest charges. I mean, when you're done paying off the loan, you're going to feel as though you need a new arm and a leg from working so hard just to pay off the loan. Frankly, I cannot recommend going that route. One thing I will say is this:

Save money when you have the opportunity to or else you will not stop regretting it. Why pay interest on a loan when you could've saved your money in the past? Do your best to avoid putting yourself in that situation and you will thank yourself for the rest of your life.

You don't have to be a circus clown to learn how to juggle. With time moving at a fast pace, life comes at you fast and you better be ready for it. Juggling work and school is no easy task; I should know. How? Let's take a look. Individuals who don't have to worry about what's in their bank account usually earn their degrees and graduate sooner than those who have to balance work and school. While working and going to school, you obviously have a lot on your plate and can't take as many classes as you'd like. Your class schedule depends on your work schedule.

Unfortunately, your day doesn't end there. After work, you have to worry about going to school and having enough energy to pay attention to the class lecture. Some people might have to attend class before going to work, and some people might have to attend class after work. Whatever the case is, it's definitely a challenge regardless of how you look at it. Lack of sleep and all-nighters are no stranger if you work and study. It doesn't end there, though. You feel tired the next day and barely have any "fuel in the tank" to get through the day but you still do, miraculously. I know, I've been there. As for the students who don't have to worry about work, I'm sure you feel like a million bucks right about now. To tell you the truth, I've been on both sides of the fence and I have to admit that neither lifestyle was easy. However, if you were to ask me which one I hated the most, I would choose the working and going to school lifestyle. I didn't enjoy the fact that I had to go to work the next day half awake just because I didn't get enough sleep the night before. Hate is such a strong word, though. Instead, let's replace it with dislike, shall we?

Let me ask you this: What if I told you that you would have a better chance of finding a job after graduating if you held down a job while you were attending school? I'm not familiar with the statistics on this matter but from what

I've heard, a lot of students have a hard time finding the job they imagined working straight out of college without any related work experience. Based on this, employers usually favor candidates who have both a degree and work experience. By bringing education and work experience to the table, they know that you're always up for a challenge. They know that you've already proven yourself and have expressed some type of leadership by taking initiative of your goals. These employers want you to bring that same type of attitude with you to work every day.

I actually had a couple of friends who I met at school and they were business majors, just like me. They always used to tell me how they were going to become company managers right after they got their degrees. Well, they graduated earlier than I did, and it turned out that they were forced to get a job flipping burgers because they weren't able to get the job they wanted. They didn't have any work experience so that might've been it. Now, I'm not trying to say that this is the case for every single college graduate but it's definitely something that you should keep in mind. Yes, when you try to juggle both work and school, it does take longer to graduate and it is going to be a little more difficult, but it will pay off in the end with your good effort. Isn't that what you want? Think about it.

What's surprising to me is that I've been seeing a lot of older adults and parents in my classes. The curious person that I am, I decided to ask why they were going to school. Their answers: Some of them said that they had been laid-off from work and wanted to use their time wisely by attending school and working towards a degree. Some of the others said that their employers refuse to promote them until they earned a degree related to their current job. If anything, this goes to show how the job market has changed over the years. Competition is more fierce than ever and employers are expecting a lot more from their current and potential employees. Is this a sign of things to come?

It seems as if having a Bachelor's or Master's degree alone isn't enough to get the job you want without some related work experience. After all, unemployment rates are through the roof in some states and competition is stiff. Unemployed people with years of work experience and multiple degrees are willing to work for less than what they used to get paid in order to make ends meet and support their families. No one said life was fair but there's only so much someone can take.

Due to current economic conditions, more and more people are looking for ways to improve their résumés and that includes earning a degree. If this is any indication of the future job market, we must be well prepared. We're going to have to make a lot of sacrifices just to maintain a decent quality of living. The good news is that we're all in the same boat, regardless of age. If you're experiencing tough times right now, you're not alone. Unfortunately, it's going to get worse before it gets better. Stay motivated and keep in mind that there's always a light at the end of tunnel. From my experience, hard work always pays off especially when you're in a sink or swim type of situation.

If you're a parent and debating whether or not you should go back to school, I would highly recommend doing so, even if it means taking a couple of classes at a local community college. Having trouble finding a babysitter? No problem! Make sure you look into the childcare services program at the school you're planning on attending. There are a lot of free services funded by the government so be sure to take advantage of them. You will be graduating before you know it.

If you're a high school graduate and debating whether or not you should take a break from school, my opinion is that you shouldn't. If you feel that you're ready for college, go head first and apply. Manage your time wisely and take advantage of your time especially if you're living with your parents or relatives who are able to support you. The world around us is changing daily and therefore, use your time to gain an edge rather than others gaining an edge on you.

If you're an unemployed full-time student, I would highly recommend finding a part-time job or internship that is related to your field of study. For example, if you want to become a nurse after you graduate, some hospitals offer internships to students. Most internships don't pay because they're assuming that you're a volunteer expecting to gain work experience. Sometimes, you have to look at the bigger picture. Gaining work experience as an intern tips the scale in your favor and you're better off than not having any work experience at all. Again, your experiences may vary but I'm generally speaking here.

If you're a student and earning a living, I say keep up the hard work and don't quit. The minute you quit on yourself is the minute you lose. Keep your head up because as long as you work hard, you have better days ahead of you. All those days that you feel exhausted and the nights with little to no sleep are going to pay off sooner than you think. Don't feel as though you're unlucky because you have to balance work and school while some of your friends don't have to. At the end of the day, you might need that work experience to land the job of your dreams. Remember, if there's a will, there's a way and winners don't make excuses, they always find a way to make it happen.

6
Making the Grade

Everyone knows how important grades are. As students, we spent countless hours working on homework and studying for tests while being isolated in a small area. We lose a lot of sleep knowing that there's a lot at stake and consequences will be paid if we don't perform the way we're supposed to. Okay, so it might not be that dramatic but we do know that grades are important. Grades are a representation of our work ethic when we apply to four-year colleges, whether it's from a high school or community college. We are judged based on our grades. If our GPA's aren't up to par, we are considered as underachievers. If our GPA's exceed expectations, then we are considered as overachievers.

Grades can be the difference between getting admitted into one of the top schools in the country or the school at the bottom of the list. Not only are our learning abilities being tested against the school's standards but our work ethic might be questioned at times as well. That's the reason why some of us lose sleep thinking about our grades while some of us sleep like babies because grades are the least of our worries. Sometimes, things don't go our way. We bring our "A game" but sometimes, we run into an instructor that we just can't get along with and that prevents us from getting the grades we deserve. Only in a perfect world would every single instructor be in complete harmony with his or her students. Our parents add fuel to the fire by setting their own high expectations.

What if I told you that you need more than just good grades to get into the school of your dreams? What if I told you that grades aren't as important as you think they are? Wait, don't pull out the party blowers just yet. In this chapter, you're going to find out whether or not you're ready to pursue higher education and how to choose a major.

Before we discuss the importance of having a college degree in today's world, I want you to determine whether or not you're "college ready". Many students drop out of college after realizing that they're not mentally prepared for it. Also, they don't know what to expect to gain from college. In some cases, these students are not fully aware of what their interests are let alone use that interest to make a living. Their decision to pursue higher education is based on their parents' and friends' advice. They would probably be better off taking a break after high school in order to find themselves and do some soul searching.

As for me, college wasn't on my radar when I was in high school. All I could think of was graduating and start making money. I wanted to work for a company that allowed me to grow within the company and eventually move up the ranks. I wanted to become the CEO of a Fortune 500 company.

It wasn't until three years after I graduated from high school that I learned the importance of having a college degree. If I wanted to survive, let alone succeed in the business world, I needed to attend college and hit the books. I'm happy to say that I will be graduating and transferring to a four-year college four months from now. I'm looking forward to applying the knowledge I gained from my studies and using it to take my professional career to whole different level.

Just how important is it having a college degree these days? Let's take a look, shall we? Long gone are the days where you can walk into the workplace of your choice and get hired on the spot. The hiring manager would know a lot about you just by judging your appearance, personality, and how you carry yourself. More and more companies are currently switching to electronic job applications. What does this mean? Well, since you're going to be submitting your employment application online, you're going to be judged by what's on your résumé and your résumé only. You're being compared to the other applicants who are competing for the same job opening.

Let's say a hiring manager has two résumés in front of him/her. Both of the résumés are nearly identical in terms of work experience except for the fact that one of the applicants has a college degree and the other doesn't. Guess who's getting the job? I'm sure you know the answer to that. That's the reason why it's more important than ever to have a college degree. In the past, it was an option. You wouldn't need a college degree to make a living and raise a family; a high school diploma was sufficient. Now, having a college degree is a must if you want to keep your lights on and water running. The world around us is changing daily and if we're not prepared for these changes, we will have to face the music. If you believe you're ready for college, it would be in your best interest to start as soon as possible in order to stay one step ahead of your competition. Just how competitive is it out there? Let's just put it this way: There aren't enough jobs to go around for everyone. It's survival of the fittest at its best.

Many students transfer to four-year colleges straight from high school. However, it seems as though they put a lot of thought into it before they actually come to a decision. They cannot decide whether they should go to a community college and then transfer as a junior, or transfer as a freshman straight out of high school. They exhaust all of their options, rightfully so. After all, it is a very serious decision that will follow them for the rest of their lives. However, they might not be aware of the options and resources available to them before they actually transfer; no need to point fingers.

The most important aspect, in my opinion, is that they're not aware of how scholarships work. I'm sure most high school students have heard about scholarships but are they familiar with the requirements? Scholarship committees offer scholarships to various students but each scholarship is only offered to students with certain qualifications. Usually, a student with the right balance of good grades, community service, and extra curricular activities is in the running for a scholarship. Also, one of the things to remember when writing a letter to a scholarship committee is to avoid expressing a need for their money due to personal financial hardships. From my understanding, that will decrease your chances of receiving the scholarship award. It makes sense when you think about it. I mean, they already know that you're in need of financial assistance or else you wouldn't have applied for the scholarship in the first place. What you want to focus on is how you would take advantage of the scholarship, if received, by making a difference in your life and the lives of others. Keep in mind that, just like you, many other students are in the same boat in need of the same scholarship. Think about how you can set yourself apart from the other applicants. Usually, the essay questions pertaining to scholarship applications will ask you where you see yourself either at a certain age or within a certain period of time.

I'm currently in the process of transferring to a four-year college myself. If I can take away one thing I learned from my counselor, it was when she told me how not a lot of students apply for some scholarships. Some of them are hesitant because they find it time-consuming and tedious. In some cases, students are awarded with scholarships just for applying, regardless of the quality of their essays. Take this with a grain of salt, though. Many scholarship foundations are established in order to help students succeed in life by gaining higher education. These scholarship committees want to give the money to deserving students, not hang onto them. As long as there is money up for grabs, there's no reason why you shouldn't take the time and give yourself a shot. After all, it's a chance to earn free money!

Over the years, community colleges have earned somewhat of a bad reputation. Students who are planning to transfer directly to a four-year college from high school see community colleges as a place of failure. Usually, high school students who didn't earn good grades would attend community colleges. Students who earned good grades in high school believed that they have worked hard enough to transfer to a four-year college. How about this, though? What if you've been admitted to a four-year college but don't have a scholarship? Have you ever thought about how you're going to pay for tuition? Are you going to turn to student loans?

Tuition isn't cheap and schools are raising tuition almost every semester/quarter. By attending a community college, you would save a lot of money. Financial assistance is available to those who qualify such as fee waivers and federal grants. The federal grants are not loans; you don't have to repay them.

Also, the good thing is that you would be taking the same courses as you would at a four-year college. When you're ready to graduate, all you would have to do is have your transcripts mailed to the school you're going to transfer to and you should receive credit for the courses you completed. Depending on the schools in your area, there's a limit of how many units/credits you can transfer to a four-year college. If you're aware of the limit, it wouldn't be a bad idea to take some of the lower-level courses at a community college along with your general education classes. Being a business major, I decided to take the lower-level business courses at my community college in order to save money. And yeah, I saved A LOT of money. I'd say somewhere in the ballpark of $2,000.

One more benefit of attending a community college is the fact that community colleges offer smaller class sizes. As you may have already figured it out by now, I didn't transfer to a four-year college directly from high school and I don't regret it one bit. Some of my friends who currently attend a four-year college complain about the large class sizes. You're basically in a room along with 200 to 300 other students learning the same subject. No problem? Alright, do you have a question? From what my friends tell me, it's nearly impossible to get in contact with the instructor. Usually, there are teacher aids walking around the classroom, who you will have to rely on to answer your questions and assist you with the subject if you don't understand the lecture or missed something. With this being said, I'm not sure if it's a classroom anymore; more like an auditorium. On the contrary, when you're in class at a community college, your chances of getting a hold of the instructor are much better. You're in a classroom along with 40 to 60 other students (depending on the course) and you can always talk to the instructor after class. Some instructors even go the extra mile by providing their e-mail address to students who need to contact them outside of class. Without a doubt, this enhances and adds value to your learning experience. Be careful though, make sure you don't forward that joke of the day e-mail to your instructor.

At the end of the day, whether you're transferring to a four-year college from high school or a community college, you will be earning the same degree as everyone else. You will be competing for the same jobs as everyone else. You owe it yourself to consider attending a community college. I met a lot of people at school who did really well in high school but wanted to attend a community college because of everything they have to offer. Now, everyone is entitled to their own opinion and not everyone will decide to take the same route. You know what? That's perfectly fine. I just want to make sure that you're making an informed decision and are aware of all the options that are available to you. It's very crucial that you do your research and figure out what's right for you. There is a gold mine of information at your disposal online and be sure to take advantage of it.

If you're a student in California, you are well aware of the difficulty in registering for the classes you need. Due to state budget cuts, class availability is very limited. Many students are not able to "add" into a class during the first week. If you've been in this situation, you're not alone. I can definitely feel your pain. One of the most important things you have to do is to keep an open mind. Let's say that you weren't able to enroll in the classes you needed, right? How about looking into other local community colleges that offer the same classes. They might be a little further in distance but you never know what might happen unless you try. You have to keep your options open. This not only applies to students from California but throughout the entire country.

Now is the time where you really have to explore your options. In my experience, I learned that you might have to go beyond your boundaries, which includes transferring to an out-of-state school. That might be exciting for some but it can also seem unideal to others. I was planning on transferring to a California State University during the Spring 2013 semester. Unfortunately, they decided that they were not going to admit any new students during that semester. What am I supposed to do? Wait around and allow time to pass me by? I remember speaking to one of my professors about this issue and he recommended that I look into schools outside of California. I found a couple of schools that I would be interested in transferring to. When you're doing research on various schools, be sure to look for the out-of-state tuition. Tuition is usually higher for students that are transferring from a different state due to non-resident fees. If you don't have some type of a scholarship, tuition can be costly. In addition to your research, it would be a smart move to schedule a campus visit. If you have your heart set on a certain school or having a hard time choosing the right school, it would be a good idea to check out their campus in-person and get a feel for it.

In addition to community colleges and out of state schools, you have a couple more options such as private colleges and online schools. When it comes to private colleges, make sure that they offer classes for your major. Also, private colleges tend to carry a hefty price tag. Don't let that discourage you, though. You might find something that you love about them such as the atmosphere, the campus, and so forth. Here's the kicker: In some cases, courses taken at a private college are not transferrable to other schools. I would highly recommend looking into this before you pull the trigger and transfer. It all depends on what your plans are. If you're planning on attending the same school for all of your educational goals, then this might not be a problem. However, if you're planning on attending a private college short-term and want to transfer at some point, then you really have to do your research or look elsewhere.

As for online schools, they're definitely not one size fits all. Even though they market themselves as the ideal school for working students, some of these online schools have campuses and you can actually take some of the courses in-person. Similar to private colleges, tuition isn't going to be cheap and the credits might not be transferrable. However, if you're looking for the convenience of an online school due to your busy schedule, attending an online school might seem very appealing to you. One thing I have to point out is that some employers do not consider online schools as traditional schools. I remember I found some information about this when I was looking into attending an online school. Be sure to conduct some research on your field of study and career path you're interested in. After spending all that time and money, you want to be confident with what's on your résumé.

Are you in the process of choosing your major? If so, then you're in the right place. Many students, just like you, are indecisive with their major and more often than not, they end up deciding on a major that they're not truly interested in. After all, you can't transfer without knowing what your major is. Here are a few tips in determining your major: What's a popular major right now? Nursing? You got it. Better yet, let's use the medical field as an example. The reason why I chose the medical field is because a lot of people determine to make a living out of it and when it's time to start working, they realize that it's not something they pictured themselves doing for the rest of their lives. For example, let's say you spend four to five years earning everything you need to become a nurse such as degrees and licenses. You're now finally ready to start working and get your hands dirty, so to speak. You found a job at a local hospital that pays well and meets all of your expectations. After working for a couple of weeks, you realize that you cannot stand the working environment. You're not a fan of being surrounded by ill patients who demand your attention and constantly call for your assistance. Frankly, they're driving you nuts. Basically, you can't take it anymore and you want out. Sure, no problem. All you have to do is accept the fact that you cannot use a time machine to rewind time in order to get back all the time you spent working so hard. But more importantly, you can't forget about your student loans. Unfortunately, student loans do not come with a refund policy and therefore, you're stuck with them until they're paid off. This may sound crazy but it happens to a lot of people every day and you just don't know it. This is why I brought this up. Choosing the right major is the most important decision of your educational career, in my opinion. It has the power to either make or break a huge chunk of your time. Also, who wants to get stuck with paying for something that they're not going to be able to utilize, right?

Before I give you some tips on how you can avoid putting yourself in that situation, I want to use another example. This time around, let's say you're a music major. You work hard and earn your degree, right? Life is good right now. You're doing a few gigs here and there at local spots. Now, here's the curveball: In order to promote your album, you realize that you need to go on tour and present your album to as many people as you can. You're the type of person that isn't too fond of traveling. You learn that some of your favorite musicians became famous and well-known not because they hoped and wished for it but they toured throughout the world and built a large fan base. You want to follow in their footsteps but in order to do this, you need to go on tours. Your decision is that you hate traveling and therefore, you choose to not become a musician.

Some of you may argue that if this person was very passionate about music, they wouldn't quit. They would stay motivated and shoot for the stars. That's exactly the point I'm trying to make. When you're cboosing a major, make sure you have a passion for it. Without passion, you will most likely not become successful. Why? Passion enables you to wake up every morning and look forward to your day. If not, then you're going to be regretful and curse at yourself. A lot of people choose their majors and career paths either by what their parents want them to be or the type of job that's in demand at the moment. This is something you don't want to do. You can earn a degree and land a job with a six figure annual income but if it's something that you're not interested in, then what good is it? Plain and simple. Let's say your parents have always wanted you to become a doctor but in reality, you have a passion for breaking down motors and putting them back together. If you force yourself to become a doctor, you're most probably not going to succeed because you're more interested in how an engine works rather the human body.

For example, I've always had a passion for business. From running a business to being a salesperson, I've always enjoyed every aspect of it. Whether I'm calling the shots or presenting a product to a potential client, I do it with a smile on my face because at the end of the day, I know that I'm enjoying my job. I look forward to meeting new people every day and learning something new. The great thing about meeting new people is that you make connections. I know that they trust me with my product recommendation and that's a rewarding feeling. Networking plays a huge role. You know what they say, "It's not what you know but who you know." Can't argue with that logic.

I promised you a few tips on how to avoid or at least reduce your chances of ending up in a ditch and here they are: First, find your passion as I mentioned earlier. This is a good place to start. Second, see what types of careers there are that are somehow related to your passion. You're not always going to find a career that meets your expectations. For example, you're all about learning the human mind and human behaviors so you decide to major in Psychology. Hypothetically speaking, you do your research and come across information that convinces you not to become a psychologist. How about exploring your options? Try looking into Business Marketing. You tell yourself that you're not a business savvy person but honestly, psychology has a lot to do with Business Marketing. Ultimately, businesses spend millions of dollars doing research on how humans react to certain things. They're spending all this money to gain information on how they're going to advertise their product. Ever wondered why music at most grocery stores and shopping malls are so calm and relaxing? That type of music isn't being played because it's a hit record. You're hearing it because it's relaxing and allows you to feel comfortable; they want you to make yourself at home. Businesses want you to spend money and earn your patronage. This might've shocked you but that's reality. Truth of the matter is that companies spend a fortune on developing and manufacturing products and the last thing they want is for that product to come up short. No one likes to lose money, especially businesses. That's what they are there for, to make money.

Finally, you have found your passion and know what to do. Let's go back to nursing and music. I know I've been picking on them a lot but they're good examples. Let's say you're interested in becoming a nurse, correct? Make a few phone calls to a few local hospitals and see if they're hiring any interns. If so, then take advantage of it. I know for a fact that a lot of people shy away from internships because unlike a job, they don't pay. However, they might be worth your while in the long run. Instead of receiving a paycheck, you could be saving yourself from drowning in student loans. Thanks to the internship, you realize that being a nurse isn't exactly your thing. You found out that it's totally different than what you had pictured. Even though you didn't get paid for the work you did, you just saved yourself thousands of dollars in student loans. See the difference?

Back to music majors: You realize that you have a burning passion for music and you get an internship at a local radio station. You talk to a few people there and learn that even though you love music, it's not something you see yourself doing to make a living. Instead of going to a music school and finding out four years and thousands of dollars later, you made the right decision before making a huge commitment to yourself and to student loan lenders. I know I mentioned this earlier but choosing the right major is often overlooked. If you don't choose the right major from the get-go, you could be headed in the wrong direction. Be sure to do your homework and see which major is right for you. Also, don't think about just the short-term pros and cons but the long-term ones as well. Choosing the wrong major is kind of like watching the movie all of your friends have been raving about for the past week and when you went to go see it, it fell short of your expectations. You can't get your money back nor the time you spent watching the movie. It's a lose-lose situation, unfortunately.

If you're in your thirties, fourties, or even fifties, then you most likely wouldn't have to worry about choosing a major at this point as you already chose it years ago. However, you still have to worry about transferring. Whether you're going to school for a degree to add eye candy to your résumé or to receive that promotion you've been working so hard for, you should know that transferring to a four-year college is crucial. Your boss might be telling you that an Associate's degree would be sufficient in order for you to receive that promotion you've been asking for all these years, but should you stop there? If it were me, I would definitely prepare to transfer. Yes, my job might be safe for the time being but will it be safe five to ten years from now? Will I be competing against my fellow colleagues for the same position in the company? Absolutely. Don't quote me on this but my instinct tells me that employers are looking for dedication and great work ethic when they ask you to earn a degree whether it's for a promotion or to keep your job. They want to see how big of a workload you can handle. If you can handle the workload at school, you can handle everything they throw at you at work. Also, consider this: Let's pretend that the company you work for is making cuts and calling for layoffs. Even though you have been told your position will not be impacted, should you take their word for it? Most certainly not. Having a college degree in your repertoire doesn't exactly make your career future-proof but it will put you in a better position to withstand current or future corporate turbulence.

Nowadays, you need a degree to become successful. Yes, there are some people who will become successful without walking into a classroom. However, that doesn't happen very often. This is coming from someone who didn't believe in going to school. If I told you that attending school isn't important, I would be the biggest liar. Hopefully, you were introduced to some new information and took advantage of the opportunity to learn a thing or two. The reason why I wrote this chapter is to educate as many people as I can on this matter because it's constantly, yet consistently affecting so many people. A lot of people are either getting left out because they didn't prepare themselves for this type of job market or are drowning in student loans. This should not be taken lightly, as it has a direct impact on your future and the type of lifestyle you will be able to maintain.

7
Tech-know-logic Lifestyles

Congratulations! You made it! You've climbed to the top of the mountain. I hope you've enjoyed your journey thus far. Before we start this chapter, I have a question for you: What is the main attraction in today's world? Or better yet, what's the main thing that captures our attention these days? I'll give you a minute to think about... And no, you're not on a game show. Time's up! If you guessed technology, you guessed right! Sorry, there isn't a car behind those curtains. (Insert Applause)

Oh technology, where do I start? You gave birth to so many conveniences throughout the years; lifestyles that would be impossible without you. Thanks to you, our lives have become much more comfortable. When it comes to technology, anything is possible and innovations are developed on a daily basis. It has changed the way we think, the way we communicate, the way we shop, and so much more. Technology has buttoned up and become sophisticated over the years by making gradual improvements to our lives, or has it? Is technology the best thing to ever happen to us? Are we too dependent on technology? Is it the way that the world is now headed, and would that be a good thing? What type of impact will it have in the future? Who will reign supreme and who will be left behind? But more importantly, how do we prepare for what's to come?

Take a look around you: What do you see? Is there someone near you? Are people standing or sitting around you? If so, what are they doing? Are they using any electronics? If you're reading the e-book version of this book, you're using an electronic device yourself. Technology has become so advanced over the past century. It's unbelievable!

Remember the days when you would have to go to someone's house just to have a conversation with them? Yes, there was a time when telephones didn't exist. Now, I wasn't alive during that time to experience what life was like without a telephone. When the telephone came out, some people loved it and some hated it. The people who loved it enjoyed using it due to how easy it was to communicate with someone rather walking to their house or sending them a postcard. The people who hated it were skeptical of using it for a couple reasons: The main reason was that they didn't want to become dependent on technology and they didn't want technology invading their lifestyle. They were content and satisfied with the lives they lived. They didn't mind walking a few blocks or a few miles just to have a conversation with someone; it had its own pleasure. Sure, you can say ask yourself, "What if I wanted to speak to someone that lived in a different state or a different country? How would I communicate with them?" In that case, the telephone would be a lifesaver. But, and this is a big but, how would you feel about the people who didn't need to use a telephone but still did? They wanted to use it but didn't need to because their friends and relatives lived nearby.

    This is the problem that exists in today's world. Technology has significantly impacted our lifestyles. We are surrounded by great technology that makes everything a lot easier and more convenient to use. What's a good example? Smart phones. Smart phones allow us to take control of our lives with just a single device in the palm of our hands. Or do they take control of us? Are we too dependent on smart phones and computers?

Let's take a couple of real life situations and you can draw your conclusion. What do you usually use your smart phone for? Texting? Checking e-mail? And dare I say, checking on your social network accounts? Let's talk about texting. Texting is a great way to communicate with someone. It's quick, discrete, and convenient. It also gives you privacy. If you're having a physical conversation with someone and don't want the person next to you to ease drop, you can text them. However, what happens when we text while driving? I know not everyone texts while driving but many people do and it's becoming a serious problem. People who text and drive are forced to direct their attention to their phone instead of keeping an eye on the road. What happens when you take your eyes off the road? You increase the chances of getting into an accident and that's exactly what's happening. It's become a huge problem. The sad part is, you don't have to be driving in order to put your life at risk. You can be an innocent bystander and if you're not paying attention to your surroundings, you're already putting yourself in harm's way.

What ever happened to stopping by a gas station and asking for directions? Does anyone remember that? To be honest with you, I don't. I grew up in a world where GPS units guided me every step of the way. I'm sure my parents and your parents certainly remember that. I wonder what would happen if smart phones and GPS systems didn't work for a couple days. Would it cause complete chaos? Would people in their early twenties or younger be able to figure out how to get directions in order to get from point A to point B? This is another example of how dependent we've become on technology.

It almost seems like technology does all the work for us. Does it do all the thinking, too? If so, will that have an impact on future generations? In my opinion, I think it will and here's why: Our parents and grandparents didn't grow up in an environment where they could rely on technology. I guess you can say that they learned "the hard way." Let's use the stopping by a gas station to get directions idea. Back then, if they didn't know how to get from point A to point B, they had to stop and figure it out. Either they used a map (yes, a real map) to figure out where they were or asked the first person they saw standing on a street corner. Nowadays, smart phones and other devices are capable of finding our location and providing turn-by-turn navigation. I know some of you would prefer to hitchhike rather than use an actual map. But see, that's the thing. Have we become so dependent on technology to the point where we shy away from using our brains? I can go on all day about this but I'm sure you get the idea.

In order to know where we're headed, we have to know where we're coming from. This is where history comes into play and shows off its value. I'd be the first to tell you that I cannot sit in History class. However, we have to educate ourselves about the past in order to prevent future mistakes. As a student, I never had an interest in history. I always used to tell myself, "Why do we have to learn about the past when we're living in the present?" Later, I learned that history repeats itself. There always have been, and will be, changes that affect a large group of people. For example, remember the Great Depression in the 1920's? We're experiencing a similar environment of financial struggles in 2012. The stock market crashed during the Great Depression era, and it crashed about five years ago as well. Technology has been the same way but not as depressing. It has always impacted the way we live and it always will.

Speaking of learning about the past, prior to the industrial revolution, technology existed but not in the same form as today. Just to give you an idea of how fast technology has grown over the past century, remember the first automobile? Yeah, it wasn't created until the early 1900's. That's only about 100 years ago. Back then, a lot of things were done by hand and had value. Cars were hand built, clothes were hand sewn, food was prepared with our hands. Mass production is a product of industrialization and consumer demand. It revolutionized the way goods were prepared and sold. You started seeing many goods used in our daily lives being produced in large quantities. How was this achieved? Technology, of course. Factories were built and they were home to many machines that produced some of the same products that we use today. This allowed production to be more efficient and with mass production, companies were able to purchase their resources at wholesale prices. This reduced their overall cost to produce each product and increased their profits. It was a win-win situation. However, what happens when human employees are replaced with machines to do their jobs? What happens when these machines are able to produce a lot more within the same amount of time than their counterparts? Will companies keep these employees? They may keep some, but not all. Why? There's no demand for them. The company who hired these employees doesn't need all the manpower they once did; machines are capable of completing the same task at a lower cost. If you've taken economics, you know exactly what I'm talking about. Some of the terms that would be relevant here are long-term costs, short-term costs, average variable cost, total average cost, margin profit, etc.

Let's use a term most of us are familiar with: supply and demand. You don't have to be an economics major to know what that means. Take a look around you: What do you see? I'm assuming you have a computer, a cell phone, and a few other things. Where did you buy them? Did you buy them from a local store or an online retailer? Where did these products come from? Who manufactured them? Chances are they were produced outside of the U.S. In order to meet the increase in consumer demand, more and more businesses are starting to produce their supply in foreign countries, mainly China. While this might be good news for consumers, it has had a significant impact on our job market. What about the jobs that are lost when these companies outsource their production outside of our country? Why are companies outsourcing their production outside of the United States? Is it to increase profit?

Now that we've covered how products are made, let's talk about the products themselves.

What are the most popular devices in today's market? Which companies design and produce these products? What type of consumers are these products marketed to? Mobile devices such as smart phones (cell phones), tablets, laptops, you name it. While many adults buy these products, the vast majority of the consumers of these products are us, young adults and college students. We have to have the latest and greatest devices. We have to make sure that we are using the newest device on the market to keep up with the most recent trends and impress our friends, nonetheless.

Let's shift gears a little bit. What about the companies that are making millions of dollars from our purchases? I guess you can say that it's a fair trade because they develop cool new products for us to play with but let's be realistic here and look at the bigger picture. These companies are making a lot of money, correct? Have you ever seen them donate funds to a charity or a good cause? Correct me if I'm wrong but do these companies participate in any type of community service? Do they have a program where their employees can take time off from work in order to do some type of community service? Let me know if you're aware of this.

By outsourcing their production to foreign countries, employment opportunities are decreasing in the U.S. Is this any indication of what's to come within the next decade or two? Are we moving towards a global economy? If you're wondering why companies are relocating their production, it's because people in foreign countries are willing to produce the same product for less. How? Labor costs. People in China are willing to work for less, much less, in order to make a living and provide for their families.

Now, in terms of quality, we don't know if quality is affected by this; it's a very controversial topic. Some people will tell you that products produced or assembled outside of the U.S. are not on the same level "quality wise" as they would be if they were produced here in the U.S. There are two sides to every argument and that's definitely the case here.

By purchasing products from companies who outsource their production, are we [consumers] encouraging these companies to continue eliminating jobs in the U.S. and move them overseas? After all, they have to meet our demand for their products, right? You might think that this is irrelevant but with the way this is going, it's going to have a huge impact on how we make a living down the road. If jobs are slowly starting to disappear, what types of jobs will be available in the future? Which job fields will be in demand? Would it be a good idea to earn a degree that will be relevant ten to twenty years from now? This raises a lot of questions and this topic should be not taken lightly. Our future is at stake here and you should be aware of it. During a global economy, we would have to compete for jobs either here in the U.S. or overseas against other applicants from countries outside of the U.S. In my opinion, not being prepared for this would be a very scary thought. How do you prepare for something like this? Work experience and education would come into play. Knowledge in a specific field or subject wouldn't hurt either.

In what other ways has technology influenced our job market? It's directly connected to how we run our errands and make our purchases. So, let's say you wake up tomorrow and want to watch the news with a cup of coffee before you head to work. Well, guess what? Your TV isn't powering on. Fast forward a few hours later and you find yourself at your local electronics store after work. You head over to the television department and you are mesmerized by all the colors and wonderful selection they offer. After speaking to a sales representative, you finally make your decision on which television set you're going to purchase.

Just for kicks, let's say the advertised price of the television is $800. Now, you're having second thoughts because you have great photographic memory and remember seeing the same television set online for $200 less. After spending an hour or two with the sales representative, you inform him or her of your decision and go home without a new television. The minute you get home, you find the same television online for $600 and you order it. All in a day's work, right? Maybe. What about the sales representative who didn't get the sale after spending all that time with you? You're probably saying, "Well, that's their job. That's what they get paid to do." Many companies are under pressure right now because they're not where they need to be financially. These companies have established sales goals in which they expect their employees to meet. If they don't, their employees might face consequences that could potentially result in reduction of hours or in some cases, termination.

With that being said, let's talk about how online retailers are able to offer lower prices compared to your local electronics stores. You might be under the impression that the prices at the electronics store down the street are outrageous. Naturally, a business that has a store with employees is generally going to have more expenses than a business that is selling their products online. If you're a business owner, you have to worry about paying rent, utilities, payroll, etc. If you're an online retailer, you might be storing your inventory in your garage or wherever you have space in your house and that would be perfectly fine. It's cost effective and time efficient. Since owning a physical store has more costs, they have to sell their products at higher prices in order to keep the lights on and still make a profit for themselves. So, it's not that their prices are high, they just have costs that an online retailer does not have. Technology allows us to make purchases online conveniently and sellers decide to take advantage of it by offering lower prices. Do we want our future landscape to consist of online retailers and online retailers only? You might want to think about that before you make your next online purchase.

    One of the major companies that filed for bankruptcy last year was a company that specialized in movie and video game rentals. Why? They weren't able keep up with the competition. It's not so much of finding a better way to do business but they became a victim of innovations in technology. Its competitors were offering the same movie and video game rentals for much less at a fixed monthly price. How are they supposed to compete when they have more costs than their competitors? Since they couldn't compete, they were forced to go out of business. Consumers are starting to rent movies and video games for as little as $1 per day. The only problem with that is they're renting it through a machine and since it's a machine, there's no contact with a human employee. But people don't pay attention to that because it's such a bargain. Companies usually have to train and pay employee salaries. With machines, all they have to do is just buy the machine and repair it when it malfunctions.

Unfortunately, when companies go out of business, it doesn't stop there. Many employees are forced to find a new way to make a living. On the other hand, struggling companies make drastic changes and the first place they usually start to cut costs is their workforce. How do they decide which employees need to be sent home? Let's take a look. For example, let's say you have to make a deposit into your checking account. You're standing outside and you see a long line inside, you don't want to wait. You decide to use an ATM. If it wasn't for technology, there wouldn't be any ATMs. You would have to wait in line just like everyone else. Due to technology, it offers conveniences and those conveniences come at a cost. By using an ATM, you're potentially contributing to the job loss of at least one employee inside that bank, specifically a teller. What happens when many people use an ATM? The demand for tellers decrease while the use of ATMs increase. When companies don't see a need for a resource, they see it as an opportunity to cut costs. Not every bank is going to let go of their tellers but we might see some banks starting to do this. If anything, tellers might not be working as many hours as they used to.

Let's use another example. Let's say you've sold a few items online and need to ship them, right? Okay, how you are going to ship them? Are you going to walk into your local post office and wait in line to mail your shipments or are you going to use one of the free online services to create and print a shipping label? Most people would probably choose the online service. However, what happens to the employees that are being paid to create those shipments at the post office? The more people use these online services, the shorter the lines will be inside the post office. As a result, the demand for these employees has decreased and I'm sure you already know what the end result is based on the example above.

There are a lot of examples I can use but I think you get the idea. Why did I bring this up in this book? I strongly believe that we are currently living in a time when everything around us is changing. The last time there was such a big change similar to what we're witnessing now was probably during the Great Depression era. It almost seems like technology has dominated our lifestyles no matter where we go or what we do.

While technology is exciting and the possibilities are endless, it's kind of like sitting on a seesaw. When one side goes up, the other must come down. As technology matures, the bigger of an impact it's going to have on our lives. I mean, who knows, we might be living in a world where we won't have any brick and mortar stores to make purchases from, just online. That proves how powerful technology really is.

It wasn't too long ago when websites were only used for viewing content, not interacting with them. Nowadays, you interact with them by making purchases and creating an account with your information. I guess it's safe to say that technology has grown up. Only in a perfect world would we have great technological advancements without any consequences, though. The more purchases we make online, the more it affects our job market. Our jobs are being replaced by machines as we speak. What types of machines? Automated Transaction Machines (ATMs), movie rental machines, self check-out machines at grocery stores and so forth. What can we do about this? While we can't rewind time, we have the present and the future in front of us. Maybe we need to have an "old school" mindset and do things that we would've done if technology didn't exist. Maybe it's a good idea to go inside the bank and have a teller process your deposit instead of the machine. Or maybe go to the post office and wait in line for a few minutes and save someone's job. You never know what might happen. This is our world and we're living in it, so let's take a control of it. If you don't take action, who will?

www.ingramcontent.com/pod-product-compliance
Lightning Source LLC
Chambersburg PA
CBHW070926010526
44110CB00056B/2166